# The Power of Walking Away

*A Journey Back to Yourself*

## Evelyn Marlowe

Blue Shoes Publishing

Published by
**Blue Shoes Publishing**

First Edition 2026

# TABLE OF CONTENTS

# INTRODUCTION

You didn't leave because you were weak.
You left because something inside of you
finally got tired of shrinking.

There comes a moment—quiet, almost
invisible—when you realize you've been
holding on to something that has not been
holding you back.
Not fully.
Not honestly.
Not in the way love is supposed to feel.

You told yourself stories.

Maybe they'll change.
Maybe they didn't mean it.
Maybe if I just love harder… they'll see me.

But love is not something you earn by
proving your worth.
And it's not something that grows in
confusion.

This book is not about walking away from people.

It's about walking away from:

- the version of yourself that settles

- the patterns that keep you stuck

- the hope that something broken will suddenly become whole

Because the truth is…
You cannot build a life on potential.

You can only build it on truth.

And sometimes the most powerful thing you can do…
is leave.

Not loudly.
Not dramatically.

But clearly.
And completely.

# CHAPTER 1: The Moment You Realize

It never happens the way you think it will.

There's no dramatic ending.
No final argument that makes everything clear.
No single moment where everything falls apart all at once.

It's quieter than that.

So quiet, you almost miss it.

It doesn't come with shouting.
It doesn't come with tears at first.
It comes in the stillness—when you're no longer reacting, no longer chasing, no longer trying to make sense of something that has never made sense.

It's the moment you stop defending them in your own mind.

You stop rewriting their behavior to make it easier to accept.
You stop telling yourself, *"They didn't mean it like that."*
You stop filling in the gaps with excuses that were never yours to carry.

It's the moment you notice how tired you feel after every conversation.

Not just physically tired—but emotionally drained.
Like every interaction costs you something.
Like you walk away feeling smaller, quieter, less certain of yourself than you were before.

You begin to notice the weight of it.

The way your energy shifts before they even speak.
The way your body tightens when their

name appears on your phone.

The way you prepare yourself—just in case.

Just in case they pull away again.

Just in case they say something that leaves you questioning yourself.

Just in case you have to explain, once again, why you deserve consistency, respect, or honesty.

And slowly… you start to ask yourself a different question.

Not *"How do I make this work?"*
But *"Why am I working so hard for something that doesn't feel right?"*

That's when the realization begins.

It's the moment you realize you've been explaining your worth instead of living it.

You've been proving yourself in spaces where you were meant to simply be accepted.

You've been over-communicating your
needs to someone who hears you—but
doesn't truly listen.

You've been showing up fully, hoping they
would meet you there.

But they don't.

And deep down… you know they won't.

You begin to see the pattern.

Not the version you hoped for.
Not the one you told yourself could exist.

But the one that has been there all along.

You give.
They take.
You wait.
They disappear.
You hope.
Nothing changes.

At first, you try to ignore it.

You tell yourself it's temporary.
That people go through things.
That relationships aren't always easy.

And that's true.

But there's a difference between something
being difficult…
and something being consistently one-sided.

You begin to see how much of yourself
you've been pouring into something that has
never been steady.

How often you've silenced your instincts to
keep the peace.
How often you've accepted less because you
didn't want to lose what little you had.

And then… something inside of you shifts.

Not all at once.

Not in a dramatic, life-changing declaration.

But gently.

Quietly.

Clearly.

You stop reacting the same way.

The things that once pulled you in… don't
have the same hold anymore.
The silence that once made you anxious…
begins to feel like space.
The confusion that once kept you stuck…
starts to feel like clarity.

You don't feel the need to chase.

You don't feel the urgency to fix it.

You don't feel the pull to explain yourself
again.

Because for the first time… you're not
trying to change the situation.

You're seeing it.

Fully.

And that kind of clarity doesn't leave room for denial.

It doesn't allow you to go back to who you were before you saw the truth.

Because once you see it…
you can't unsee it.

And that's where everything changes.

Not anger.
Not even sadness.

Just clarity.

A quiet understanding that settles into your chest.

This isn't what I want.
This isn't what I deserve.
This isn't going to change.

And clarity doesn't rush you.

It doesn't force you to act immediately.
It doesn't demand a dramatic exit.

It simply stays with you…
until you're ready to listen.

Until you're ready to choose differently.

Until you're ready to stop betraying yourself
just to hold on to something that was never
holding you.

That moment—the moment you realize—is
not the end.

It's the beginning.

The beginning of honesty.
The beginning of self-respect.
The beginning of something that finally
feels like peace.

Because clarity…
changes everything.

# CHAPTER 2: You Stayed Longer Than You Should Have

You didn't stay because you were weak.

You stayed because you believed.

And belief can be a beautiful thing—
when it's rooted in truth.

But when belief is tied to potential instead of
reality…
it can keep you in places that slowly take
you away from yourself.

You believed in them.

Not just who they were…
but who they could be.

You saw the glimpses.

The moments where they were kind.
Present.
Attentive.

The version of them that made you feel
chosen.

And you held onto that.

You held onto it even when it became
inconsistent.
Even when it became rare.
Even when it started to feel like something
you had to earn instead of something that
was freely given.

You believed in their words.

The promises.
The apologies.
The *"I'll do better."*

And maybe they meant it in the moment.

Maybe they truly believed they would
change.

But words without action don't build trust.

They create hope.

And hope—when it's not supported by consistency—can keep you waiting longer than you should.

You believed in the version of them you saw in the beginning.

The beginning is where everything feels easy.

Where attention flows.
Where effort feels natural.
Where connection feels real.

And that version of them felt safe.

It felt like something worth holding onto.

So when things changed…
you didn't let go.

You tried to get back to that version.

You thought, *"If I just love them the right way… if I just give it time… if I just stay patient… we can get back to that."*

But the truth is:

The beginning is not always who someone
is.

Sometimes it's who they are when it's easy.

And who they are when it's difficult…
is who you have to learn to see clearly.

But belief without consistency becomes self-
abandonment.

And that's the part no one talks about.

Because from the outside, it looks like
loyalty.
It looks like patience.
It looks like love.

But inside…
it feels like something else.

It feels like ignoring your own needs.
Silencing your instincts.

Convincing yourself to accept things that don't sit right in your spirit.

You kept giving chances.

Not because you didn't see the truth…
but because you hoped the next chance
would be different.

You told yourself:
"This time they'll follow through."
"This time they understand."
"This time things will change."

And each time…
you gave a little more of yourself.

More time.
More understanding.
More emotional space.

Until one day, you realize…

You've been the one doing all the adjusting.

You've been the one carrying the weight of the relationship.
You've been the one making room for behavior that doesn't make room for you.

And still… you stayed.

Because leaving didn't feel easy.

Leaving meant letting go of the belief.
Letting go of the hope.
Letting go of what you thought this could become.

And that kind of loss…
isn't always about the person.

It's about the future you imagined with them.

But here's the truth that changes everything:

People don't change because you stay.

They don't grow because you give more.
They don't become consistent because you are patient.

Change is a decision.

A personal one.

And it requires effort that no one else can give for them.

You cannot love someone into becoming who they need to be.

You cannot stay long enough to create a version of them that doesn't exist yet.

And you cannot sacrifice yourself in the process of waiting.

Because the longer you stay in something that isn't meeting you…
the further you move away from what would.

There's a moment—just like in the chapter before—

where you begin to see this clearly.

You stop asking, *"What if they change?"*
And start asking, *"Why haven't they already?"*

You stop focusing on their potential…
and start recognizing their pattern.

And that's where the shift begins.

Not in anger.
Not in blame.

But in honesty.

You begin to understand that staying longer didn't make you stronger.

It made you more disconnected from yourself.

But that doesn't make you wrong.

It makes you human.

You loved.
You believed.
You gave.

And now…
you're learning.

Learning that love without consistency is confusion.
Learning that patience without boundaries is self-neglect.
Learning that belief must be matched with reality.

And most importantly—

Learning that you don't have to stay where you are not being met.

Because love should not feel like something you have to convince yourself of.

And the right connection…

won't require you to stay longer than you should just to feel it.

# CHAPTER 3: The Cost of Holding On

Every time you stayed when you should have left…
you paid a price.

Not always visible.
Not always immediate.

But real.

The kind of cost that doesn't show up all at once.
The kind that builds slowly, quietly—until one day, you feel it everywhere.

In your thoughts.
In your body.
In the way you move through your life.

You lost:

- time
- energy
- peace
- parts of yourself

Time you can't get back.

Time spent waiting.
Wondering.
Hoping things would shift.

Time you could have been growing…
healing… becoming.

Instead, you were pausing your life—
holding space for something that wasn't
holding space for you.

You lost energy.

Not just physical energy—but emotional
energy.

The kind it takes to:
explain yourself
replay conversations
analyze every word, every silence

The kind it takes to keep showing up…
when deep down, you're already tired.

You became exhausted in a way that sleep
couldn't fix.

Because it wasn't your body that needed
rest.

It was your heart.

You lost peace.

The kind of peace that comes from feeling safe.
The kind that allows you to relax… to trust… to just be.

Instead, you lived in uncertainty.

You didn't know where you stood.
You didn't know what would happen next.
You didn't know if things would be good—
or if something would shift again.

And that kind of instability…
slowly becomes your normal.

You start calling it "love."

But it's not love.

It's emotional inconsistency.

And over time…
it begins to take more than it gives.

You lost parts of yourself.

And this is the cost that hurts the most.

Because you don't always notice it right away.

It happens slowly.

You start adjusting.

Becoming more patient.
More understanding.
More forgiving.

Until one day, you realize…

You've adjusted so much…
you barely recognize yourself.

You started questioning your instincts.

The things that once felt clear…
now feel confusing.

You second-guess yourself.

*"Am I overreacting?"*
*"Maybe I'm expecting too much."*
*"Maybe this is normal."*

But your instincts were never wrong.

They were just ignored.

Silenced.

Pushed aside in favor of keeping something
alive…
that was already showing signs of breaking.

You started doubting your needs.

The things you once knew you deserved:
consistency
communication
effort

…started to feel like too much to ask for.

So you minimized them.

You told yourself:
"I don't need that much."
"I can handle this."
"It's not that bad."

But it was.

Because every time you lowered your
needs…
you lowered your experience of love.

You lowered your standards.

Not all at once.

But little by little.

You accepted things you once said you
never would.
You tolerated behavior that once would have
been a clear boundary.

Not because you didn't know better.

But because you were trying to make it work.

Trying to keep something together…
that required you to slowly fall apart.

And slowly…

you forgot what it felt like to feel secure.

You forgot what it felt like to feel:
chosen
safe
at ease

You became used to:
waiting
wondering
adjusting

You became familiar with emotional uncertainty.

And unfamiliar with peace.

That's what holding on does.

It doesn't just keep you connected to them.

It keeps you disconnected from yourself.

Disconnected from your voice.
Your truth.
Your boundaries.

Disconnected from the version of you…
that doesn't have to question whether they
are enough.

Because you are enough.

You always were.

But staying in something that doesn't reflect
that…
can make you forget.

And that's the real cost.

Not just what you lost in the relationship—

But what you lost within yourself.

The confidence.
The clarity.
The certainty.

The quiet knowing that says:
*This feels right.*

But here's the part that matters most:

Just because you paid the cost…
doesn't mean you have to keep paying it.

Awareness changes everything.

The moment you begin to see what it has
taken from you…
is the moment you begin to take yourself
back.

Your time.
Your energy.
Your peace.
Your self.

Because holding on is not always love.

Sometimes…
it's fear.

Sometimes…
it's habit.

Sometimes…
it's the hope that things will become what
they've never been.

But once you recognize the cost…

you start asking a different question.

Not *"How do I keep this?"*

But—

*"Is this worth losing myself?"*

And the answer…
when you're honest with yourself—

is no.

# CHAPTER 4: Walking Away Is Not Giving Up

Walking away is not failure.

It's not weakness.
It's not losing.

It's choosing yourself.

And for a long time…
that may not have felt like an option.

Because somewhere along the way, you were taught that staying meant strength.
That enduring meant love.
That holding on—no matter how heavy it became—was something to be proud of.

So when the thought of leaving began to surface…
it didn't feel empowering.

It felt like giving up.

Like you didn't try hard enough.
Like you didn't love deeply enough.
Like maybe, if you had just done a little more… things could have been different.

But that's not the truth.

The truth is:

You tried.
You showed up.
You gave.

And at some point, you realized…
you were the only one doing it.

Walking away is not about quitting on
someone.

It's about refusing to quit on yourself.

It's recognizing that:

• love should not feel like confusion
• consistency should not feel rare
• respect should not feel earned

Love is not meant to leave you guessing.

It's not meant to feel like a puzzle you have
to solve or a problem you have to fix.

It's meant to feel clear.

Steady.

Safe.

And when it doesn't—when it becomes
something you constantly have to question,
explain, or chase—
that's not love growing.

That's you adapting to something that isn't
meeting you.

Consistency should not feel rare.

It should not feel like something you
celebrate when it happens… because it
happens so infrequently.

Consistency is not a reward.

It's a foundation.

It's what allows trust to build.
What allows connection to deepen.
What allows you to relax into the
relationship instead of constantly bracing for
what might come next.

And respect… should never feel like
something you have to earn.

You should not have to prove your worth in
order to be treated with care.

You should not have to explain why your feelings matter.

You should not have to shrink yourself just to maintain peace.

Respect is not conditional.

And the moment it becomes something you have to fight for…
is the moment you have to begin questioning where you are.

Walking away is the moment you stop trying to fix something that is not yours to fix.

Because that's what you've been doing.

Trying to understand them.
Trying to help them.
Trying to love them into becoming someone who could meet you.

But people are not projects.

And love is not a place where you are meant to constantly repair what someone else is unwilling to change.

You cannot fix inconsistency.
You cannot fix emotional unavailability.
You cannot fix someone who does not see
the need to grow.

And more importantly—

It is not your responsibility to try.

Walking away is the moment you release
that responsibility.

Not with anger.
Not with resentment.

But with clarity.

A quiet understanding that says:

*This is not mine to carry anymore.*

And in that moment… something shifts.

Because when you stop trying to fix them…

you finally have the space to focus on
yourself.

And that's where the rebuilding begins.

And start rebuilding what is.

Not what you hoped for.
Not what you imagined.

But what is real.

You begin to rebuild your sense of self.

The parts of you that were overlooked…
start to come back into focus.

Your voice becomes clearer.
Your boundaries become stronger.
Your needs become non-negotiable.

You begin to rebuild your peace.

The constant overthinking begins to quiet.
The emotional highs and lows begin to
settle.
The space that once felt empty… begins to
feel calm.

You begin to rebuild your trust in yourself.

You start listening to your instincts again.
Honoring what feels right… and walking
away from what doesn't.

Not second-guessing.
Not explaining.

Just knowing.

And perhaps most importantly…

You begin to rebuild your understanding of
love.

You start to see that love is not supposed to
feel like struggle.
It's not supposed to feel like waiting.
It's not supposed to feel like something you
have to earn.

Love—real love—meets you.

It doesn't confuse you.
It doesn't drain you.
It doesn't make you question your worth.

Walking away doesn't mean you didn't care.

It means you care enough about yourself…
to no longer stay in something that hurts.

And that is not giving up.

That is growth.

That is strength.

That is self-respect.

Because sometimes…

the most powerful thing you can do
is not hold on tighter—

but let go…
and choose yourself.

# CHAPTER 5: Breaking the Emotional Attachment

You weren't just attached to them.

If it were only about the person…
it would have been easier to let go.

But it wasn't.

You were attached to:

- the memories
- the potential
- the hope

And each of those holds a different kind of
weight.

The memories…

They don't leave easily.

They replay at unexpected times—
in quiet moments, in familiar places, in
songs you didn't realize were tied to them.

You remember how it felt in the beginning.

The laughter.
The connection.
The way things seemed effortless.

You remember the moments that made you
feel seen.

And those moments become anchors.

Because when things started to shift…
you didn't forget how it once felt.

You held onto that version.

You told yourself:
*"It was real."*
*"We had something."*
*"It wasn't always like this."*

And you're right.

It wasn't always like this.

But memories don't define what something
is.

They only remind you of what it once was.

And sometimes…
what it once was is no longer what it is.

Then there's the potential.

The version of them you believed they could
become.

The version that:
communicates clearly
shows up consistently
chooses you without hesitation

You saw it in glimpses.

Just enough to make it feel possible.

And that's what made it so hard to let go.

Because you weren't holding onto who they
were.

You were holding onto who you believed
they could be.

But potential is not reality.

And staying connected to someone based on
who they *might* become…
keeps you stuck in a future that may never
arrive.

You end up loving an idea.

Waiting for something that isn't fully
present.

And in the process…
you delay your own life.

But the hardest attachment of all…
is hope.

Hope doesn't feel like something you should
let go of.

It feels like something you should hold onto.

Protect.
Believe in.

Hope whispers:

*"Maybe this time will be different."*
*"Maybe they've changed."*
*"Maybe they just need more time."*

And every time something almost shifts…
hope grows stronger.

Every small effort feels like progress.
Every moment of connection feels like
confirmation.

You start to believe:
*"This is it… this is where it turns around."*

But then… it doesn't.

And instead of letting go, hope tells you to
try again.

To wait a little longer.
To give a little more.

And before you realize it…
you're no longer holding onto the
relationship.

You're holding onto hope.

And hope, when it's not grounded in truth…
can keep you emotionally attached far
longer than love ever could.

Breaking the emotional attachment is not
about forgetting them.

It's about seeing clearly.

It's about separating:
what was real
from what you wished was real

It's about recognizing that:
memories are not a foundation
potential is not a promise
hope is not a guarantee

And that kind of clarity…
doesn't come all at once.

It comes in layers.

There will be moments where you feel
strong.
Clear.
Certain.

And then moments where something pulls
you back.

A memory.
A thought.
A feeling you thought had passed.

That doesn't mean you're not healing.

It means you're human.

Because emotional attachment isn't just
mental—it's felt.

It lives in your body.

In the way your heart responds.
In the way your mind drifts.
In the way certain feelings linger longer than
you expect.

And breaking that attachment takes time.

Not force.
Not denial.

But truth.

Because healing begins when you replace
hope with truth.

Not what you wish was happening.

But what actually is.

Not:
*"Maybe they'll change."*

But:
*"They haven't."*

Not:
*"Maybe this could work."*

But:
*"It hasn't been working."*

Not:
*"Maybe I just need to be patient."*

But:
*"I've already been patient."*

Truth can feel harsh at first.

It doesn't comfort you the way hope does.

It doesn't soften the reality.

But it frees you.

Because truth removes the illusion.

And without the illusion…
you can finally see the situation for what it
is.

Not what you hoped it would become.

And when you see clearly…
the attachment begins to loosen.

Not because you stopped caring.

But because you stopped pretending.

You stopped holding onto something that
required you to ignore yourself.

You stopped feeding a connection that was
not feeding you.

And slowly…
you begin to return to yourself.

Your energy shifts.

Your thoughts become quieter.

The emotional pull becomes less intense.

Not gone completely…
but no longer controlling you.

And one day, you realize something:

You're no longer waiting.

You're no longer hoping.

You're no longer holding on.

You're moving forward.

And that's how you know…

the attachment has begun to break.

# CHAPTER 6: The Fear of Being Alone

Sometimes we don't stay because we love them.

We stay because we're afraid of what comes after.

Not the person…

but the space they leave behind.

Silence.

Space.

Starting over.

And those three things can feel overwhelming when you've been used to filling your life with someone else's presence—even if that presence was inconsistent.

Because even inconsistency…

can feel familiar.

And familiarity feels safer than the unknown.

So you stay.

Not because it feels right…

but because leaving feels uncertain.

You start to imagine what life would look
like without them.

No more messages.

No more waiting.

No more moments—good or bad—to look
forward to.

Just… quiet.

And that quiet can feel heavy at first.

Because when everything slows down…

you're left alone with your thoughts.

Your feelings.

Your truth.

And that can be uncomfortable.

Because there's no distraction anymore.

No one to focus on.

No emotional highs and lows pulling your
attention away from yourself.

Just you.

And for many people…

that's the part they're trying to avoid.

Not being alone in a physical sense—

But being alone with themselves.

Because in that space, questions come up:

*Why did I stay so long?*

*Why did I accept so little?*

*Why did I ignore what I felt?*

And those questions don't always have easy
answers.

So instead of facing them…

you stay in something familiar.

Even when it's not fulfilling.

Even when it's draining.

Even when it's slowly taking more from you
than it gives.

Because starting over feels harder.

But here's the truth:

Being alone is not the same as being lonely.

Loneliness is not about who is around you.

It's about how connected you feel.

And you can be in a relationship…

and still feel completely alone.

You can be talking to someone every day…

and still feel unseen.

You can be giving your time, your energy,

your presence…

and still feel like it's not being received.

That is loneliness.

Not the absence of people—

but the absence of connection.

And staying somewhere you are not

valued…

is the deepest form of loneliness there is.

Because you are there.

You are present.

You are trying.

And still…

you are not being met.

There's a quiet pain in that.

The kind that doesn't always show on the

outside.

But you feel it.

In the moments where you hesitate to speak your truth.

In the moments where you accept less just to keep the peace.

In the moments where you realize you are giving more than you are receiving.

And slowly…

you begin to shrink.

Not intentionally.

But gradually.

You make yourself smaller to fit into something that was never meant to hold you fully.

And that's where the fear keeps you stuck.

Because leaving means facing that emptiness.

Facing the quiet.

Facing yourself.

But what you don't realize—at least not yet—is that the space you're afraid of…

is the space where you begin to return to
yourself.
The silence you fear…
is where your thoughts become clear.
The space you're avoiding…
is where your peace begins.
And starting over…
is not starting from nothing.
It's starting from truth.
From awareness.
From experience.
From a deeper understanding of what you
will and will not accept.
Starting over is not a step back.
It's a step forward—
into a life that is no longer built on
confusion.
And yes, it will feel unfamiliar at first.
There will be moments where you miss the
routine.

The connection.

Even the person.

Not because it was right…

but because it was known.

But with time… something shifts.

The silence becomes less heavy.

The space becomes less empty.

The quiet becomes something you begin to appreciate.

You start to feel your own presence again.

Your own thoughts.

Your own energy.

Your own sense of self.

You begin to realize…

you were never truly afraid of being alone.

You were afraid of letting go.

Afraid of what it meant.

Afraid of what you would have to face.

Afraid of what would come next.

But what comes next…

is you.

Not the version of you that was adjusting.

Not the version of you that was waiting.

But the version of you that is whole.

That is grounded.

That is clear.

That no longer confuses attention with

connection…

or presence with love.

And when you begin to experience that…

being alone no longer feels like something

to fear.

It feels like something to protect.

Because in that space…

you are no longer lonely.

You are connected to yourself.

And that changes everything.

# CHAPTER 7: Letting Go of the "Maybe"

"Maybe they'll change."

"Maybe they'll come back."

"Maybe this isn't the end."

Maybe.

Such a small word…

but it holds so much power.

Because maybe doesn't ask you to decide.

It doesn't force you to move forward.

It doesn't require you to let go.

It simply keeps you… in between.

Not fully holding on.

Not fully letting go.

Just waiting.

And waiting can feel like progress when you're not ready to face the truth.

Because as long as there's a "maybe"…

there's still hope.

And as long as there's hope…

you don't have to accept what is.

You don't have to grieve it.

You don't have to release it.

You don't have to close the door.

You can stay in that space where everything

still feels possible.

But that space…

is also where people stay stuck.

Because maybe keeps you attached to a

future that hasn't happened…

while keeping you disconnected from the

present that is already here.

You begin to build your life around

possibilities.

Not reality.

You replay conversations.

You look for signs.

You hold onto moments that feel like they

mean something more.

You start asking:

*What if they reach out?*

*What if things change?*

*What if this isn't over?*

And those questions keep you emotionally tied…

even when physically, things have already shifted.

But your life cannot move forward on uncertainty.

You cannot build something solid on something that is undefined.

You cannot grow in a space where everything feels conditional.

You cannot find peace…

while constantly waiting for something that may never come.

At some point, you have to stop asking what could happen…

and start acknowledging what is happening.

Not what you wish were true.

Not what feels easier to believe.

But what is real.

What has been shown to you… consistently.

Because patterns don't lie.

And clarity doesn't come from waiting.

It comes from seeing.

Seeing clearly.

Without the filter of hope.

Without the comfort of "maybe."

Just truth.

And truth… can feel uncomfortable at first.

Because it asks you to accept something you may not be ready to accept.

It asks you to let go of possibilities that once felt real.

It asks you to release the version of the story you wanted to believe.

But truth also frees you.

Because once you stop holding onto "maybe"…

you stop holding yourself back.

You stop delaying your own life.

You stop putting your future on pause…
waiting for someone else to decide if they
want to be part of it.
And that's where clarity begins.
Clarity requires decision.
Not a perfect decision.
Not a decision without emotion.
But a decision rooted in truth.
A decision that says:
*This is what it is.*
*This is what it has been.*
*This is what I need to accept.*
And decision requires courage.
Because choosing clarity means letting go of
comfort.
Letting go of the unknown that still feels
safe…
because it hasn't fully ended yet.
It means closing a door that you once hoped
would stay open.

It means releasing control over something
you never truly had control over.

And that's not easy.

There will be moments where you want to
go back.

Back to wondering.

Back to hoping.

Back to holding onto the possibility.

Because "maybe" feels softer than truth.

It feels less final.

Less heavy.

But it also keeps you stuck.

And staying stuck comes at a cost.

The cost of your peace.

The cost of your growth.

The cost of your ability to move forward
into something that is real…

something that is certain…

something that meets you fully.

Letting go of "maybe" doesn't mean you
didn't care.

It doesn't mean what you felt wasn't real.

It means you are choosing to live in reality…

instead of waiting in possibility.

It means you are choosing clarity over confusion.

Truth over illusion.

Movement over stagnation.

And that choice…

is where your life begins to shift.

Because once you let go of "maybe"…

you make space for what is meant for you.

Not something uncertain.

Not something inconsistent.

But something clear.

Something steady.

Something that doesn't require you to question where you stand.

And that is what you deserve.

Not a "maybe."

But a knowing.

A certainty.

A connection that doesn't leave you
waiting…
but meets you where you are.
Fully.
And freely.

# CHAPTER 8: Rebuilding Your Self-Worth

When you've been in something that diminished you…

you don't just walk away from them.

You have to come back to yourself.

And that part…

is often harder than leaving.

Because leaving is a moment.

But returning to yourself…

is a process.

It doesn't happen overnight.

It doesn't happen just because you made the decision to walk away.

It happens slowly.

In the quiet moments.

In the space that once felt unfamiliar.

In the absence of what used to occupy your time, your thoughts, your energy.

You begin to notice what's left.

And at first…

it may feel like something is missing.

Because for so long, your focus was on

them.

On the relationship.

On what was happening—or not happening.

So when that's no longer there…

you're left with yourself.

And that can feel unfamiliar.

Because somewhere along the way,

you stopped prioritizing who you are.

You adapted.

Adjusted.

Compromised.

Until parts of you became quieter.

Less visible.

Less certain.

So coming back to yourself…

means rediscovering what was always there.

You relearn:

• what you deserve

• what feels right

• what you will no longer tolerate

And that relearning takes honesty.

Because for a while, your sense of what you deserved may have shifted.

You may have accepted less than you needed.

You may have tolerated behavior that once would have been a clear boundary.

Not because you didn't know better—

but because you were trying to make something work.

Trying to hold onto something you believed in.

But now…

you get to redefine that.

You begin to ask yourself:

*What does respect look like to me?*

*What does consistency feel like?*

*What kind of connection allows me to feel*
*safe, seen, and valued?*
And as you ask those questions…
you begin to remember.
You remember that you are not meant to
question your worth.
You remember that your needs are not too
much.
You remember that love should not require
you to shrink.
You relearn what feels right.
Not based on what someone else gives
you—
but based on what your body, your mind,
and your spirit recognize as truth.
You start paying attention to how things
feel.
Not just what is said.
Not just what is promised.
But what is consistent.
What is steady.

What allows you to feel at ease… instead of on edge.

You begin to trust that feeling again.

The quiet knowing inside of you that says:

*This feels right.*

Or…

*This doesn't.*

And instead of ignoring it—

you honor it.

That's where self-worth begins to rebuild.

Not in big, dramatic changes.

But in small, intentional choices.

You relearn what you will no longer tolerate.

And this is where your boundaries begin to take shape.

Not as walls—

but as clarity.

Clarity about what you accept.

Clarity about what you walk away from.

Clarity about what aligns with who you are
becoming.
Because self-worth is not just about
knowing your value.
It's about protecting it.
It's about no longer allowing situations that
diminish you to remain in your life.
Even if they feel familiar.
Even if they once meant something to you.
And that can be uncomfortable at first.
Because setting boundaries means choosing
yourself…
even when it's difficult.
Even when it means disappointing someone.
Even when it means letting go again.
But every time you choose yourself—
your self-worth strengthens.
Every time you walk away from something
that doesn't align—
you reinforce your value.
Every time you listen to your instincts—

you rebuild trust in yourself.

Self-worth is not something they give you.

It's not something someone else creates.

It's not something you earn through being

enough for someone else.

It's something you reclaim.

Piece by piece.

Moment by moment.

Choice by choice.

You reclaim it when you stop chasing

validation.

You reclaim it when you stop explaining

your worth.

You reclaim it when you no longer settle for

less than what you know you deserve.

And over time…

something shifts.

You no longer feel the need to prove

yourself.

You no longer feel the need to overextend

just to be seen.

You no longer feel the pull toward situations
that once felt normal… but were never
healthy.
Because you've come back to yourself.
And that changes everything.
You begin to move differently.
You choose differently.
You recognize sooner.
You walk away faster.
Not from fear—
but from clarity.
Because when you know your worth…
you don't have to question where you stand.
You don't have to convince anyone to see
you.
You don't have to remain in places that
require you to forget who you are.
Rebuilding your self-worth is not about
becoming someone new.
It's about returning to who you were…
before you started settling.

Before you started doubting.

Before you started adjusting to something

that didn't reflect your value.

And once you return to that place…

you don't lose it again.

Because now you know:

Your worth was never the problem.

You just needed to come back to it.

# CHAPTER 9: Healing Without Closure

You may never get the apology.

The explanation.

The closure.

And that can be one of the hardest truths to accept.

Because a part of you still wants understanding.

You want to know:

*Why did this happen?*

*What changed?*

*Did it ever mean what I thought it did?*

You want something that brings clarity to the confusion.

Something that makes it all make sense.

And for a while…

you may wait for that.

You may replay conversations in your mind.

Search for answers in their behavior.

Look for signs that explain what you
experienced.
You may even hope that one day…
they'll come back and say the things you
needed to hear.
"I'm sorry."
"I understand now."
"You deserved better."
And maybe they will.
But many times…
they won't.
Not because you didn't deserve it.
But because not everyone has the
awareness…
or the willingness…
to take accountability for what they've done.
And that's where healing becomes your
responsibility.
Not in a heavy way.
But in an empowering one.

Because if your healing depends on them—
on what they say… on what they do… on
whether they come back—
then your peace remains tied to someone
who has already shown you
they cannot give you what you need.
And that keeps you stuck.
Waiting.
Hoping.
Holding on to the idea that closure will
come from them.
But closure is not something they give you.
It's something you create.
And creating closure doesn't mean
pretending it didn't matter.
It doesn't mean minimizing what you felt.
It doesn't mean forcing yourself to "move
on" before you're ready.
It means choosing to accept what is…
even without the answers.

It means recognizing that:

you may never fully understand their behavior

you may never get the words you were hoping for

you may never receive the acknowledgment you deserve

And deciding…

to move forward anyway.

Through acceptance.

Acceptance is not agreement.

It's not saying:

"This was okay."

"This didn't hurt."

"This didn't matter."

It's saying:

*This happened.*

*This is what it was.*

*And I cannot change it.*

Acceptance allows you to stop fighting reality.

Because for a long time, that's what you've
been doing.
Fighting what is…
by focusing on what you wish it had been.
But once you accept it—
you begin to release the resistance.
And with that…
comes a sense of calm.
Through truth.
Not the version of the story you created to
make it easier to stay.
But the version that is grounded in reality.
The truth about how you were treated.
The truth about how it made you feel.
The truth about what was missing.
Because clarity comes when you stop
rewriting the narrative…
and start seeing it as it was.
Not worse than it was.
Not better than it was.
Just real.

And truth…
even when it's uncomfortable—
sets you free.
Through letting go.
Letting go doesn't mean you forget.
It doesn't mean you stop caring instantly.
It doesn't mean the feelings disappear
overnight.
Letting go means releasing your attachment
to needing something from them.
Needing an explanation.
Needing an apology.
Needing closure.
Because the more you need those things…
the more your healing remains dependent on
someone else.
And healing…
is something you deserve to have control
over.
Letting go means you stop waiting.

You stop looking for signs.

You stop hoping for a conversation that may never happen.

You stop placing your peace in their hands.

And you bring it back to yourself.

Where it has always belonged.

There will be moments where it feels unfinished.

Where you wish you had one more conversation.

One more chance to say what you needed to say.

That's normal.

Because humans seek resolution.

We want things to feel complete.

But not everything ends with clarity.

Not everything closes neatly.

Some things end in silence.

Some things end without explanation.

And part of healing…

is learning to be okay with that.

Not because you didn't deserve more.
But because you are no longer willing to
wait for it.
You begin to understand that closure is not a
moment.
It's a decision.
A decision to:
stop replaying the past
stop searching for answers
stop holding onto what cannot be changed
And instead…
choose yourself.
Choose your peace.
Choose your healing.
Choose your forward movement.
Because closure doesn't come from them
saying the right thing.
It comes from you deciding:
*I have everything I need to move on.*
And when you reach that place—
something shifts.

The questions become quieter.

The need for answers becomes less intense.

The attachment begins to loosen.

Not because you got what you wanted—

but because you no longer need it.

And that's when you know…

you've created your own closure.

# CHAPTER 10: Choosing Peace Over Chaos

Peace feels unfamiliar when you've been used to emotional highs and lows.

When you've been in something that kept you on edge—

where moments of connection were followed by distance,

where clarity was followed by confusion,

where presence was followed by absence—

your nervous system begins to adjust to that rhythm.

It begins to expect it.

You start to anticipate the shifts.

You learn to read into silence.

You prepare yourself for inconsistency.

And over time…

chaos starts to feel normal.

Not comfortable—

but familiar.

So when peace enters your life…

it doesn't always feel right at first.

It feels quiet.

Too quiet.

There's no tension to resolve.

No emotional rollercoaster to ride.

No guessing what the other person is

thinking or feeling.

Just… stillness.

And that stillness can feel unfamiliar.

Because you're not used to it.

You may even find yourself questioning it.

*"Is something missing?"*

*"Why does this feel so calm?"*

*"Shouldn't there be more intensity?"*

But what you're experiencing…

is not something missing.

It's something different.

Peace.

And peace is not boring.

It's stable.

It's knowing where you stand.
It's not having to question someone's
intentions.
It's not feeling the need to analyze every
interaction.
It's consistency.
The kind that doesn't need to be earned.
The kind that doesn't come and go.
The kind that allows you to trust what
you're experiencing… without second-
guessing it.
It's safe.
Not in a limiting way—
but in a grounding way.
Safe enough to be yourself.
Safe enough to express your needs.
Safe enough to exist without feeling like you
have to perform, prove, or protect yourself
constantly.
It's grounded.

There are no emotional spikes pulling you in different directions.

No highs that make you feel everything…
followed by lows that leave you questioning everything.

Just a steady presence.

A connection that builds… instead of fluctuates.

And that kind of peace…
takes adjustment.

Because when you've been conditioned to associate love with intensity—
peace can feel unfamiliar at first.

But unfamiliar does not mean wrong.

It means you are experiencing something new.

Something healthier.

Something that doesn't require you to lose yourself in order to keep it.

Choosing peace is not about settling.

It's about elevating your standard.

It's about recognizing that love does not need chaos to feel real.

It does not need inconsistency to feel exciting.

It does not need confusion to feel deep.

Because real depth…

is found in stability.

Real connection…

is found in consistency.

Real love…

is found in peace.

And once you begin to experience that… something shifts within you.

You no longer crave the emotional highs.

You no longer feel drawn to situations that keep you guessing.

You no longer mistake intensity for connection.

Because you've felt the difference.

You've felt what it's like to be at ease.

To not carry the weight of uncertainty.

To not question your place in someone's
life.

To not feel the need to overextend just to
maintain something.

And once you experience that…

you begin to protect it.

You become more aware of what disrupts
your peace.

More intentional about what you allow into
your life.

More selective about the energy you engage
with.

Not out of fear—

but out of clarity.

Because you understand now:

Peace is not something you stumble into.

It's something you choose.

Every day.

In the people you allow.

In the boundaries you set.

In the situations you walk away from.

You choose peace when you stop
entertaining confusion.

You choose peace when you no longer chase
inconsistency.

You choose peace when you trust yourself
enough to walk away from what doesn't feel
right.

And that choice…

becomes a lifestyle.

A way of moving through your life with
intention.

A way of protecting your energy.

Your time.

Your emotional well-being.

Because you've learned—

peace is not something to question.

It's something to recognize.

To honor.

To hold onto.

And once you experience it…

you will never want chaos again.

Not because chaos no longer exists—

but because you no longer accept it.

You no longer confuse it with love.

You no longer allow it to define your

experience.

You choose differently.

You live differently.

You love differently.

And in that choice…

you find something that chaos could never

give you.

Peace that stays.

# CHAPTER 11: Becoming Someone Who Doesn't Settle

This is where everything changes.

Not on the outside first…
but within you.

It's not a dramatic shift that happens
overnight.
It's not a sudden moment where everything
feels perfect and clear.

It's quieter than that.

It's a series of decisions.

Small ones at first.
Then stronger ones.

Until one day…
you realize you're no longer the same
person you used to be.

You stop chasing.

Not because you don't care.

But because you understand that what is
meant for you…

does not require pursuit that feels like
exhaustion.

You no longer feel the need to reach out
first,
to follow up,
to keep something alive that isn't being
nurtured on both sides.

You stop overextending your energy just to
maintain a connection.

Because you've learned:

If it requires constant effort just to exist…
it is not aligned.

You stop explaining.

You stop trying to make someone
understand your needs, your feelings, your
boundaries—over and over again.

Not because your needs don't matter…

But because you've realized:

The right people don't need repeated
explanations.

They listen.
They adjust.
They care.

And if someone continuously shows you
they are unwilling or unable to meet you…

you no longer try to convince them.

You accept it.

And you move accordingly.

You stop proving.

You stop proving your worth.
Your value.
Your intentions.

You stop trying to be "enough" for someone
who doesn't recognize what you already
bring.

Because you've come back to yourself.

You know who you are.

And you understand that your worth is not
something that needs validation from
someone else.

It's something you carry.

Something you embody.

Something you protect.

You become someone who:

• recognizes red flags early
• trusts their instincts
• walks away without hesitation

Recognizing red flags early doesn't mean
you judge people harshly.

It means you pay attention.

You no longer ignore what doesn't feel
right.

You no longer make excuses for behavior
that contradicts what you need.

You no longer tell yourself:

*"Maybe I'm overthinking."*
*"Maybe it's not that serious."*

Because you've learned—

what you feel matters.

And what you notice…
is worth paying attention to.

Trusting your instincts becomes your
foundation.

You stop second-guessing yourself.

You stop asking others what they think you
should do.

Because you've rebuilt your connection to
your own inner voice.

That quiet knowing inside of you that says:

*This feels right.*
Or…
*This doesn't.*

And instead of questioning it—

you follow it.

Even when it's uncomfortable.
Even when it requires you to walk away
from something you once wanted.

Because you trust yourself enough…
to know that what you're feeling is valid.

Walking away without hesitation…

doesn't mean you don't feel anything.

It doesn't mean it's easy.

It means you are no longer willing to stay in something that doesn't align with who you are becoming.

You don't wait for things to get worse.
You don't wait for more proof.
You don't wait until you are completely drained.

You act when you see enough.

Because you understand:

Delaying the decision…
only delays your peace.

And that's the shift.

Because now…
you understand something deeply:

Your peace is not negotiable.

Not for attention.
Not for potential.
Not for familiarity.

You don't trade your peace for temporary connection.

You don't sacrifice your clarity for someone else's inconsistency.

You don't abandon yourself… to keep something that doesn't feel right.

Your peace becomes your priority.

Not in a selfish way—

but in a self-respecting way.

You begin to build your life around it.

You choose relationships that support it.
You set boundaries that protect it.
You walk away from situations that disturb it.

And the more you do this…

the stronger you become.

Not hardened.

But clear.

Grounded.

Confident in your ability to choose
differently.

You no longer fear losing people.

You understand that what is not aligned…
is not meant to stay.

And what is meant for you…

will meet you where you are—
without requiring you to lose yourself in the
process.

Becoming someone who doesn't settle…

is not about being perfect.

It's about being aware.

Aware of what you deserve.
Aware of what you need.
Aware of what you will no longer accept.

And honoring that awareness…
with action.

Because growth is not just what you realize.

It's what you do with what you realize.

And once you reach this point—

you don't go back.

Not because you can't.

But because you won't.

Because now you know:

What you offer is valuable.
What you need is valid.
And what you deserve…

is real.

# CHAPTER 12: Walking Into Your Life

Walking away is not the end.

It can feel like it in the beginning.

It can feel like something has been lost.
Like a chapter has closed without the ending you expected.
Like you're stepping into something unknown… without a clear sense of what comes next.

And for a moment, that can feel heavy.

Because endings—especially the ones you didn't plan—
carry emotion.

They carry memories.
They carry meaning.
They carry the weight of what you thought something could become.

But walking away is not the end.

It's the beginning.

Not of something external first…
but of something internal.

A shift.

A return.

A new way of moving through your life.

Of:

• clarity

• confidence

• self-respect

• real love

Clarity becomes your foundation.

You no longer feel pulled in different
directions.
You no longer question what you already
know.

You see things for what they are—
not what you hope they will become.

You trust what is shown to you.
You honor what you feel.

And that clarity brings peace.

Because confusion no longer has a place to
live.

Confidence begins to grow.

Not loud.
Not forced.

But steady.

It's not about proving anything to anyone.

It's about knowing who you are…
and moving from that place.

You become more comfortable in your
decisions.

More certain in your boundaries.

More grounded in your sense of self.

Because you've walked through something
that required you to choose yourself.

And that changes how you see yourself.

Self-respect becomes non-negotiable.

You no longer stay where you are not
valued.

You no longer accept what doesn't align.

You no longer abandon your needs just to
maintain a connection.

You move differently.

You choose differently.

Not from fear—
but from awareness.

Because you understand now:

You are responsible for how you allow
yourself to be treated.

And you begin to honor that responsibility…
with intention.

And then…
real love.

Not the kind you have to question.

Not the kind that leaves you wondering
where you stand.
Not the kind that comes and goes.

But something steady.

Something clear.

Something that doesn't require you to
decode it.

Not the kind you have to fight for.

Love is not meant to feel like a battle.

It's not meant to feel like something you have to earn, prove, or hold together on your own.

It's not meant to exhaust you.

Real love meets you.

It doesn't require you to chase.
It doesn't require you to explain yourself repeatedly.
It doesn't require you to sacrifice your peace just to keep it.

It aligns with you.

And when it does…
it feels different.

It feels calm.

Grounded.

Certain.

The kind that meets you…

fully and freely.

And perhaps the most important part of this beginning…

is not what comes into your life next.

It's how you walk into your life now.

You are no longer the version of yourself
that stayed too long.
That questioned your worth.
That waited for something to change.

You are someone who has seen clearly.

Someone who has felt deeply.
Someone who has learned what it means to
choose yourself.

And now…

you carry that with you.

Into every decision.

Every connection.

Every space you allow yourself to enter.

You walk with awareness.

You walk with boundaries.

You walk with a deeper understanding of what you deserve.

And because of that…

your life begins to open in a different way.

Not because everything becomes perfect.

But because you are no longer settling.

You are no longer holding onto what doesn't align.

You are no longer building your life around uncertainty.

You are walking into something real.

Something that reflects who you are now.

And who you are now…

is someone who knows:

You don't have to chase what is meant for you.
You don't have to question what is clear.
You don't have to fight for what is aligned.

Walking away didn't take you away from your life.

It brought you back to it.

And now…

you are not starting over.

You are starting from truth.

From strength.

From self.

And that is not an ending.

That is everything.